THE LITTLE BOOK OF
ADULT

GAMES

SADIE CAYMAN

summersdale

THE LITTLE BOOK OF ADULT GAMES

This edition published 2019
First published as *Very Naughty Games* in 2011
Published as *The Little Book of Naughty Games* in 2014

An Hachette UK Company
www.hachette.co.uk

Summersdale Publishers Ltd
Part of Octopus Publishing Group Limited
Carmelite House
50 Victoria Embankment
LONDON
EC4Y 0DZ
UK

www.summersdale.com

Printed and bound in China

ISBN: 978-1-78783-003-5

Substantial discounts on bulk quantities of Summersdale books are available to corporations, professional associations and other organisations. For details contact general enquiries: telephone: +44 (0) 1243 771107 or email: enquiries@summersdale.com.

Contents

INTRODUCTION

Introduction

Boring sex lives are for your parents, vicars, that woman who runs the PTA and anyone who gets excited by a yellow-breasted cockatoo. Yours may be going through a dry patch, a rough patch, or an unusually wet patch, but no matter how much of a sexpert or novice you may be, there's no harm in spicing things up with some super-fun, super-sexy sex games.

So congratulations for picking up this book, and welcome. This sexy stocking full of titillating treats should get you hot under the collar and ready for some stripped-down, hard-core bedroom action. From frisky foreplay teasers to downright dirty duvet dalliances, there's something in here for every sexual occasion. Pay attention to the underpants difficulty ratings to get an idea of just how much fun you're in for.

So get your "f*ck me" underwear on and prepare to take it off not long after, 'cause it's time to play!

I GENERALLY
AVOID
TEMPTATION
UNLESS I CAN'T
RESIST IT.

MAE WEST

FLIRTY FUN

How to Play

You will need:
A bottle, a pair of handcuffs, a spanking tool and a bucket of ice cubes.

Difficulty:

Place the bottle in the centre of the room à la "Spin the Bottle" and position the other objects at equal distances around the circle. Take turns with your partner to spin the bottle. If it rests pointed at a "safe zone", where there are no objects, the other person takes their turn at spinning. If not, follow these rules:

If the bottle's pointed at…

… the handcuffs, cuff your partner to the nearest static object and do whatever you want to them.

… the spanking tool, your partner (or yourself, it's your choice!) gets a light spanking for their bad behaviour.

… the bucket of ice cubes, then cool your partner down with an ice cube down the back or in their underwear.

How to Play

You will need:

Water pistols, buckets, balloons and plenty of water! (Use warm water – you don't want to catch hypothermia, and avoiding shrinkage in the nether-regions is always a good thing.)

Difficulty:

Find somewhere where nudity and water sports go hand in hand – such as a back yard that's not overlooked. Dress yourself in your skimpiest underwear and a tight-fitting white T-shirt. Select your watery weapons of choice – no, boys, not that – (water pistols, water bombs, a good old-fashioned bucket) and fill them up. Take it in turns to ask each other sexy questions, to test how well you know each other: "What's my favourite position?", "Where's the craziest place we've ever had sex?", for example. For every question your partner gets wrong, you get to give them a good squirting. Keep going till your outfit is good and see-through.

How to Play

You will need:

Your own clothes, some sexy underwear, candles, rose petals, cards/envelopes and a pen. (This game involves a bit of forward planning, but it'll be worth it. That's a promise!)

Difficulty:

Before your partner arrives for your date, hide the clothes you've been wearing that day (including your underwear) in different locations around the house. Write out clues that will lead your partner from your coat, to your skirt/trousers, to your shirt, etc. and place them in envelopes with each item of clothing (the first clue to your coat is taped to the front door). The last clue (with your underwear) should lead your lover to a spot you've decided to recline naked, surrounded by rose petals and candles. They've found the pleasure chest!

> ### *Titillating Tip*
> Try to make the clues as enticing as possible to keep your partner interested, and to ensure they don't just go looking for you round the house.

MY BEST
CHAT-UP LINE?
"LET ME SHOW
YOU A FEW OF MY
JUDO HOLDS."

HONOR BLACKMAN

SEX FOR ALL SEASONS

You will need:

Twenty small pieces of paper, a pen and a box of melt-in-your-mouth chocolates.

Difficulty:

Before your partner arrives for their Valentine's treat, draw hearts on ten of the pieces of paper and place all the pieces of paper face down on the bed. Get naked. Each choose one piece of paper and turn it over. If the piece of paper has a heart on it, you must select a chocolate from the box and eat it off your partner's body. If you both pick a heart then you get double the pleasure! If neither of you pick a heart, wait until the end of the song that's playing before picking again. Use this time to get your partner hot and bothered. After each round, replace the pieces of paper and mix them up. Play until you either run out of chocolates or you'd rather be nibbling on each other.

How to Play

You will need:

Pancake batter, a shallow frying pan, a bottle of pouring syrup and two aprons.

Difficulty:

Wearing nothing but aprons, take it in turns with your partner to cook a pancake. Whoever goes first must then see how many times you can flip the pancake without dropping it. After each successful flip they receive a seductive kiss from the other person. Their turn ends when they fail to flip the pancake. If they manage to successfully flip the pancake five times in a row then they must pour syrup over the other person's naked body and lick it off. To rack up the rude rating a notch, insist that your partner flips their next pancake completely nude.

> ### *Titillating Tip*
> Don't feel like getting doused in sticky syrup? How about strawberry sauce, chocolate spread or squirty cream?

LEAD ME
NOT INTO
TEMPTATION.
I CAN FIND THE
WAY MYSELF.

RITA MAE BROWN

GOOD GIRLS GO
TO HEAVEN AND
BAD GIRLS GO
EVERYWHERE.

HELEN GURLEY BROWN

How to Play

You will need:
A tent and two sleeping bags.

Difficulty:

During your camping trip or weekend at a festival, take some time out with your partner and retreat to your tent. Zip yourselves up in your sleeping bags fully clothed and then race to see who can get naked first without getting out of the sleeping bag. Whoever can present a full pile of their clothes outside their sleeping bag first is the winner.

Raunchy Rules
Since you went to the trouble of getting yourselves naked, the winner should really receive some kind of reward. Emerge from your sleeping bags and get cosy. Whoever undressed the fastest should then receive the best oral sex EVER!

Titillating Tip
Had enough beer and boogying for one day? Text your partner or cute friend/person you just met in the crowd and invite them back to your tent for some daytime playtime.

How to Play

You will need:

A pair of handcuffs, some sexy lingerie and a blindfold.

Difficulty:

Put your sexy lingerie on under your clothes. Handcuff your naughty partner to a chair in just their underwear. Proceed to ask them to recall details about your relationship (the saucier the better). For every detail they recall correctly you will remove one item of your clothing, but if they answer incorrectly you will blindfold them, and the game will continue without them being able to enjoy the view. Any further wrong answers will result in your putting clothes back on. The game ends when the questioner has stripped bare and the captive partner can be set loose to receive their reward.

How to Play

You will need:

Lots of kinky little treats wrapped up in festive paper and a sack/pillowcase.

Difficulty:

Find a time of the day when you're alone with your partner (make sure there's no chance grandma can walk in on the game). Stuff all the presents into the sack and invite your partner to pick them out one by one. For each gift they have ten seconds to identify what is in the package but are only allowed one guess. Then they must open the gift. If they guessed right they get to keep the gift to use later in the evening. If not, then they must hand it over to you. If you're normally fairly reserved in the bedroom, throw a few random toys in there that shock you. You never know – if they guess right you might get a Christmas present you didn't expect.

BE NAUGHTY — SAVE SANTA A TRIP.

ANONYMOUS

3
♥

EAT ME!

How to Play

You will need:

Squirty cream and strawberries.

Difficulty:

Surprise your partner by preparing them a tasty dessert. Strip down and squirt cream onto your nipples, bellybutton and anywhere else that takes your fancy. While lying down on the kitchen table, carefully position strawberries on the creamy areas, and call for your lover to come in and lick you all over.

Raunchy Rules

Your partner has three minutes to eat as many strawberries as they can (while giving you a good licking in the process). For every strawberry they eat you'll give them a little lick back afterwards. And remember, not everyone's big on cream - chocolate mousse might also get them going.

Titillating Tip

If things are getting too sticky, take your naked body (and your partner) off to the shower, so they can rinse you off.

How to Play

You will need:
A few bars of chocolate, two spatulas and dice.

Difficulty:

Melt a big bowl of dark chocolate (milk, if you like, but dark's an aphrodisiac) and sit down naked in the middle of the room. Each of you will need a plastic spatula and a die. Roll the dice, and whoever gets the highest number is allowed to paint one body part of the other person. When you're both good and chocolatey, stop spreading, then whoever rolls the highest number can demand which body part the other person licks.

Raunchy Rules
For alternative game-play, ditch the spatulas and smear the chocolate on with your fingers.

Titillating Tip
Don't overdo it with the licking. Chocolate tastes good, but you don't want to make yourself sick when things could be about to get raunchy!

FANTASY MIRRORS DESIRE. IMAGINATION RESHAPES IT.

MASON COOLEY

IT'S ABSOLUTELY
UNFAIR FOR WOMEN
TO SAY THAT GUYS
ONLY WANT ONE
THING: SEX. WE
ALSO WANT FOOD.

JAROD KINTZ

HORNY HOOPLA

How to Play

You will need:
Chocolate-covered peanuts, sugar-coated chocolate buttons, canned cream and ring donuts.

Difficulty:

Strip down to your underwear and stand a few feet away from your partner. You have twenty attempts each to try and achieve all of the following:

- Throw a chocolate-covered peanut into your partner's mouth = 2 points
- Throw a sugar-coated button into your partner's mouth = 4 points
- Squirt cream onto your partner's torso = 6 points
- Land a donut anywhere on your partner's body (head, feet, resting on a boob) = 8 points

NB: Anyone who can successfully toss a donut onto their partner's penis scores 10 points for their awesome skills! (If your partner is a lady, then the 10-pointer is awarded for successful finger looping.)

SEX ON TELEVISION CAN'T HURT YOU, UNLESS YOU FALL OFF.

ANONYMOUS

LIGHTS, CAMERA, ACTION!

SEX ON SCREEN

How to Play

You will need:
A couple of your favourite sexy movies and some serious acting skills.

Difficulty:

If you've never been to drama school, this one might take a bit of practice. Have a few blush-crushing drinks and put on a sexy movie to watch together. Decide who will go first before the title sequence fades, and then when the first sexy scene appears, watch it intently, press pause and perform it on (or for) your partner. Then press play and let the movie continue.

Raunchy Rules
You set the rules for what will be included (i.e. kissing, fondling, spanking, oral sex, nudity, stripping, etc.). If either one of you doesn't want to act out a particular sequence they must forfeit by performing a task decided by their partner. (Examples include: giving the other person a foot massage, doing some kind of domestic chore or downing a shot of tequila.)

How to Play

Back in simpler times, cheeky boys and girls would perform in coin-operated booths, flashing their flesh and teasing customers each time they made a contribution. Now it's your turn to make some money and show your partner what they might get their hands on later. Make sure your lover brings their spare change along!

You will need:
A coin collection box (or make your own) and sexy music to listen to.

Difficulty:

Sit your partner on the sofa next to a conveniently placed box with a slit marked "Insert Coins Here". Put on some sexy music and wait for them to pay up. Donations of different amounts will result in different performances, which you should make your customer aware of (see next page)*. Their final amount donated will equal the number of minutes you spend pleasuring them after they're all excited and out of pocket.

How to Play

- The smallest coin you get = reveal a sexy secret about yourself.
- The next smallest coin you get = describe a sexual fantasy.
- The largest coin you get = do a sexy dance (clothed).
- The smallest note you get = flash some flesh.
- The next smallest note you get = do a sexy dance (naked).
- The largest note you get = take it to the next level – you set the mark for this one!

*These are just suggestions for what might get your partner excited. If you're a terrible dancer then you might want to come up with other ways to put on the ultimate peep show.

> ### *Titillating Tip*
> Use the money you earn to buy yourself some new sexy underwear or a sex toy for the bedroom, so you both feel the benefit!

I DON'T SAY WE ALL OUGHT TO MISBEHAVE, BUT WE OUGHT TO LOOK AS IF WE COULD.

ORSON WELLES

NO WOMAN GETS AN ORGASM FROM SHINING THE KITCHEN FLOOR.

BETTY FRIEDAN

LET'S GET PHYSICAL

How to Play

You will need:

Music that turns you on, a remote control for your music player and some chairs.

Difficulty:

Play this one in your underwear. Turn the music up and get moving. Take it in turns to hold the remote control and when you feel your partner least expects it, pause the song and dash for the nearest chair. If you sit before they do, they must perform a lap dance for a minute before you pump the music up and you both get moving again. Remember to remove a chair to make the competition more fierce!

> ### *Titillating Tip*
> Play as dirty as you can! Distract your partner when it's their turn with the remote by flashing your best body parts, gyrating up against them and throwing them off their game.

BALL SKILLS

How to Play

Boys might think they've got 'em, and girls might know how to handle a pair when the occasion suits, but this game will divide the dribblers from the drop-kickers and ultimately determine who's the best ball-buster once and for all.

You will need:

An indoor golfing green, a golf ball and a putter.

NB: if you don't have an indoor golfing green you can always improvise with a plastic cup laid on its side (tape it down), or a flat ring-shaped object like a bangle in place of the hole.

Difficulty:

Tee off! Take it in turns to run the golfing gauntlet. Count how many putts it takes you to get the ball in the hole. These equal the number of items of clothing you must remove before your partner takes their turn. The aim is to get the ball in the hole in as few shots as possible – unless you're feeling like naked might be the way to go... in that case, hit it into the rough.

Raunchy Rules

Whoever gets a hole-in-one not only wins the trophy (or a bottle of bubbly you can both share) but gets to call the shots in the bedroom!

Titillating Tip

Dress up in your sexiest golf wear – that means tight-fitting knits and mini shorts with over-the-knee socks; golfing trousers with long socks and a tartan cap. Don't forget to stick your butt out when you're lining up the shot.

YOU CAN
STAY BUT
YOUR CLOTHES
MUST GO.

ANONYMOUS

You will need:

A vibrating device, a blindfold, a poster-sized out-line of a human body (naughty bits included) and a pen.

Difficulty:

Blindfold your partner, turn them round three times and position them in front of the poster, which you've pinned up on the wall. They should now draw three circles onto the poster, hoping they've picked somewhere more exciting than your big toe. Then they may remove their blindfold, and tickle you with the vibrator in the places they circled. Then it's their turn to feel the buzz!

Raunchy Rules

If they ask for help, don't give it (unless you're trying out the tip below). If they make marks on an elbow, or even off the poster, it's their fault if you don't feel in the mood to get it on.

Titillating Tip

Guide your partner as the pen moves over the picture of the body by describing the parts they're virtually touching. If there's a certain spot that gets you going, make sure they stop there and for a change, demand they kiss/nibble/suck that spot instead.

6 ♥

HOLIDAY
HOT SPOTS

9 ♠

THE LANGUAGE
OF LUST

How to Play

Locals love it when people from out of town try to blend in. So rather than flirting in plain old English, why not try your hand at a spot of foreign-speak to spice things up?

Difficulty:

Spend the afternoon hanging out with the cute bartender at your hotel pool. Get them to teach you all translations for a couple of come-ons that'll be sure to have you hooking up with the locals. Once you've practised on your friends, smarten yourself up and head off to the bars. Some possible one-liners you might want to learn are:

¿En qué lado de mi cama prefieres dormir?
(Spanish)
Which side of my bed would you like to sleep on?

Tu es tellement chaude que tu fais fondre l'élastique de mon caleçon! **(French)**
You're so hot you melt the elastic in my underwear.

Scommetto venti euros che stai per darmi un due di picche. **(Italian)**
I bet you twenty euros you're going to turn me down.

How to Play

For every successful attempt (i.e. getting someone's number, a cheeky snog... or more!) you get a point. The person with the most points at the end of the night wins!

Raunchy Rules

A foreign chat-up line must be used at least once during each attempt. Another member of the group should hover close-by to check no cheating is taking place.

Titillating Tip

Locals love to share their culture. So, once you've bagged one, get them to teach you a chat-up line or sexy phrase of their own. For every one you can successfully repeat (and translate back into English) for your friends, award yourself a bonus point.

SEX IS A PART
OF NATURE.
I GO ALONG
WITH NATURE.

MARILYN MONROE

How to Play

Flights can be yawnsome at the best of times – what better way to liven them up than by getting in some high-altitude horny behaviour with your partner or even a hot stranger. Yes, please!

Difficulty:

Make friends with the hottest person on your flight and switch seats so you're together – this could be a challenge in itself. Once you're settled and acquainted, explain the rules to them. The aim of the game is to orgasm on the flight. This can be achieved by any means necessary, but there are four golden rules that cannot be broken:

1. You cannot spend more than five minutes away from your seat.
2. You cannot tell anyone else what is going on.
3. You cannot get caught in the act.
4. If you're unable to get off on board then you must buy your recently relieved buddy a drink from the cart.

Raunchy Rules

If you're seeing to yourself in the bathroom, your new friend's going to have to take you on trust. Why not snap a photo of you pleasuring yourself on your mobile phone to give him something sexy to look at.

Titillating Tip

A good way to ensure you're sitting next to your cutie is by befriending them at check-in. Get your seats allocated together, and start the banter before the plane's even taken off.

SEX IS LIKE AIR; IT'S NOT IMPORTANT UNLESS YOU AREN'T GETTING ANY.

JOHN CALLAHAN

How to Play

Vacations can be lazy times, so heading out into the pool or the sea is a great way to burn off some of that ice cream. Splashing around in the waves and looking like a drowned rat can be dull, though, and not particularly sexy, so this game is designed to inject a bit of sauce into your swim-time.

Difficulty:

Only play this game on a day when (or in a place where) the waters are calm. Head out into the sea with your partner to a place where you can both comfortably stand on the seabed. Once you're deep enough, and most of your body is underwater, touch a part of your own body and ask your partner to guess where they think you're touching yourself. If they get it right, they get a kiss. Then, it's their turn.

Raunchy Rules

Kisses should increase in intensity and passion with each correct answer your partner provides.

> ### *Titillating Tip*
> Try leaving your swimwear on the beach and playing the game in the nude. All the touching will probably get you both so excited you'll be writhing around like horny sea lions on the sand before you know it!

SEX IS ONE OF THE
NINE REASONS FOR
REINCARNATION.
THE OTHER EIGHT
ARE UNIMPORTANT.

HENRY MILLER

How to Play

You will need:

A period house with extensive gardens, a penchant for Jane Austen-esque dramas and some olde-worlde costumes (optional).

Difficulty:

Head to one of the country's many beautiful period homes where you're free to roam the grounds and feel like you've stepped back in time. Find secluded spots where young children and grannies feeding the ducks can't see you, and try out some of the following:

- Jump into the lake fully clothed and then emerge to passionately embrace your partner.
- Pretend one of you is a lowly servant, the other a wealthy aristocrat in need of some lower-class action.
- Pretend you're caught in a storm and take shelter in a nearby barn, remove your clothes and immediately start getting it on. Go as far as you like with this one, as long as no one's looking!

You will need:

A shopping list for each player, a wallet with cash in it and a local supermarket.

Difficulty:

Write out a shopping list of items with sexual connotations, or ones that can be used for naughty games (including some in this book). Give a list to your partner and keep one for yourself. Head to your local supermarket and agree a meeting point somewhere outside. Screech "Go!" and then the winner is the first person to find and purchase all the items and make it back to the meeting point. Items must be bought, not stolen or borrowed or from your own personal collection of portable sexy things.

> ### Titillating Tip
> To make things extra fun, dress up for the sweep. Pick a sexy theme such as burlesque.

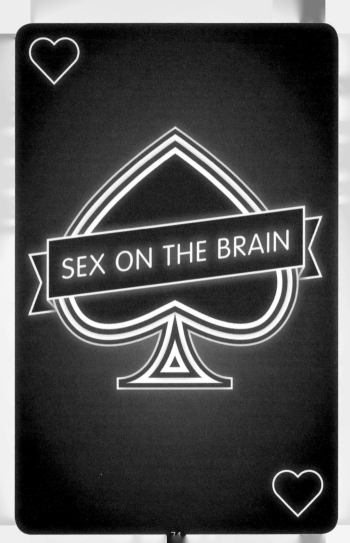

How to Play

Going out for a romantic meal is the best way to set things in motion for a night of hot adult behaviour. But why wait till you're back home before you get your partner all excited? Whet their appetite with this saucy game and they'll pay the bill just to get you home faster!

Difficulty:

Think of something really sexy. It could be your favourite sexual position, a particular sexual encounter with your partner, the part of their body you love the most, or anything that turns you on. Once you have the thought in your head, your partner gets to ask you six sexy questions (to which you can only answer yes or no) to try to decipher what you're thinking. If they guess it right, then you have to buy them dessert/a glass of wine/pay the bill, etc.

Raunchy Rules

Your partner has to trust that you're not changing your mind to avoid buying them any after-dinner treats, so don't be a sore loser – if they guess right, fess up!

Titillating Tip

Don't think just because you're in a fancy public place that touching is banned. Play footsie, and slowly run your fingers up and down your partner's hand to let them know you're thinking sexy thoughts.

SEX-RATED

How to Play

You will need:

A long coat, a pair of dark glasses and a mobile phone.

Difficulty:

The aim of the game is to successfully take something that belongs to your lover, while distracting them with your sheer sexiness. Tell them if you are successful they have to take you out for dinner. You have one day to achieve this and must complete the following steps:

1. Send this text to your lover: "We need to meet. You've been a bad boy/girl." Arrange to meet at a restaurant or bar.
2. Wear a long coat (with nothing but sexy undies underneath) and head out to meet them.
3. Arrive at your destination, sit with them and flash some leg. Tell them you have something for them in the bathroom and they should follow you there in one minute.

4. When they arrive in the bathroom, remove your jacket and throw yourself on them.
5. While they're distracted by your nakedness, make your play and take something.
6. Back at the table reveal your steal and get them to pay the bill. Hot sex and a free dinner – not bad for a day's work!

Raunchy Rules

Only you know all the steps and can know if you successfully completed them, so this is more a game for you and your libido than to be played as a pair. There's no need to actually steal anything from your lover, and you can return their property after they tell you how hot you were!

Titillating Tip
Imagine yourself as a sexy spy and try to ignore any weird looks around you. Make sure your coat is fitted and sexy and that you don't look like a kid playing dress up.

WHEN I GET
DOWN ON MY
KNEES, IT'S
NOT TO PRAY.

MADONNA

How to Play

You will need:
To have no shame.

Difficulty:

Commuting to work is one of the least sexy times of the day. No longer. Sit next to your partner on the train and obey the following rules:

1. When the train pulls into a station, start kissing your partner. You can only stop when the train starts moving again.
2. If the train goes through a tunnel you must remove one item of clothing.
3. When the announcer says the name of your destination at any point during the journey, you must touch each other as inappropriately as you dare.
4. If you visit the buffet car, or if a food cart comes by, you must order a *hot* coffee and a *warm* muffin.

Raunchy Rules

If your partner fails to comply with any of the rules, you have permission to flirt outrageously with your fellow commuters until they complete the next task.

> ### *Titillating Tip*
> Make up your own rules so the journey is even sexier - such as "no-underwear Mondays", "talk-dirty Tuesdays", "wet-shirt Wednesdays", "touch-me-up Thursdays" and "fumble Fridays"!

I CONSIDER SEX A MISDEMEANOUR. THE MORE I MISS, DE MEANER I GET.

MAE WEST

HOT UNDER
THE COLLAR

How to Play

You will need:
A wedding to attend (not yours!) and a bright/distinctive lipstick.

Difficulty:

Speeches, bad music, awkward conversation with elderly relatives – yes, weddings can be dull, but they're also a hotbed for well-dressed, horny singles looking for some action, i.e. the perfect setting to get hot under the collar. This game requires players to apply lipstick, so as long as you're down with that, you're good to go. The aim of the game is to mark as many shirt collars as you can with your lipstick.

Raunchy Rules
- Every collar you've tagged = 1 point
- Every buttonhole flower you steal = 2 points
- Every tie or bowtie you manage to swipe = 5 points
- Anyone who finishes the night wearing a top hat = 10 points
- Photographic evidence of your lipstick on a man's chest = 15 points

How to Play

You will need:
A sudoku puzzle, a pen and sparkling wine.

Difficulty:

Do you have a partner who spends far more time studying than studying you? This game will redress the balance and make sure you're all they've got their eyes on. Take a simple game of Sudoku (it helps if you know how to play this game first) and hand it to your partner – make sure you pick one that's not too easy for them. Each correct number that they insert into the puzzle corresponds to something you're going to do. Each time they insert a new number you stop doing the previous action and continue with a different one. You must keep performing the act until they insert a different number.

If they insert a:

* 1, 2 or 3: you will strut around in nothing but a pair of killer heels and your underwear.

- 4, 5 or 6: you will take off an item of their clothing.
- 7, 8 or 9: you will pour sparkling wine down yourself and let them lick it off.

NB: If you're more into puzzles than your partner, no worries, the roles can easily be reversed!

Raunchy Rules

If they complete the entire puzzle in under 15 minutes (not that it will be easy for them with you frolicking around in the nude), then they should be rewarded with some *very* hot sex.

Titillating Tip

If your partner's struggling to complete the puzzle, they're allowed to ask you for help, but only once. If you correctly insert a number, they have to put the puzzle down, take off their clothes, and give you a backrub in the nude.

IF YOU USE
THE ELECTRIC
VIBRATOR NEAR
WATER, YOU WILL
COME AND GO AT
THE SAME TIME.

LOUISE SAMMONS

How to Play

You will need:
Sexy gym kit.

Difficulty:

To win this game you have to prove your sexy status in three different stages.

Stage 1: Warm Up

Kit yourself out in your sexiest gym wear and run side by side on two treadmills. After each minute of running passes you must both make a sexy remark to your partner. It can be anything as long as it includes one of the following words: sex, body, hot, dirty, sweat. Both of you must say your sentences within ten seconds of the minute passing, so keep an eye on your treadmill timer to make sure you're being quick enough. Keep going until one of you can't think of a remark in the time limit. The other person is the winner of Stage 1 and scores one point.

Stage 2: Cool Down

Head to the mats to do some stretching. Take it in turns to decide on a stretch position for both of you. When you are stretching you have to make groaning sex noises; start quietly, and get progressively louder (you must make a louder noise than the one your partner just made). The loser is whoever cracks first. Score one point for winning.

Stage 3: Sauna

There's no point going to the gym if you're not going to get all sweaty and naked in the sauna. Whoever dares to bare all scores a point for this stage. You can both score points if you're both feeling like flashing the flesh.

Raunchy Rules

The winner is whoever scores the most points. Their reward? How about one of these:

- A relaxing back rub back home.
- A steamy shower they won't forget in a hurry.
- A glass of wine and a sexy bubble bath.

Titillating Tip

Bonus points! If either you or your partner gets chatted up by someone during the gym session, take home an extra point (and maybe someone else's number!).

If you're interested in finding out more
about our books, find us on Facebook at
Summersdale Publishers and follow us
on Twitter at **@Summersdale**.

www.summersdale.com

Image credits

Dice icon © RealVector/Shutterstock.com

Underwear icon © Shorena Tedliashvili/Shutterstock.com

Cocktail glass icon © agrion/Shutterstock.com

Playing-card suit vectors © Vitezslav Valka/Shutterstock.com